SAINT THÉRÈSE
OF LISIEUX

CTS Children's Books

Contents

A little flower 3

Pauline her 'mother' 4

Thinking of God 6

A special day 8

A gift from Jesus 10

Above all things 12

On pilgrimage 14

Like the snow 16

The Little Way 18

Thérèse and the missions 20

The sleep of Christ 22

Some of Thérèse's thoughts 24

Text by Silvia Vecchini
Illustrations by Antonio Vincenti
Translated by Simone Finaldi

Saint Thérèse of Lisieux: Published 2009 by the Incorporated Catholic Truth Society, 40-46 Harleyford Road, London SE11 5AY. Tel: 020 7640 0042; Fax: 020 7640 0046; www.cts-online.org.uk. Copyright © 2009 The Incorporated Catholic Truth Society in this English-language edition.

ISBN: 978 1 86082 594 1   CTS Code CH 23

Translated from the original Italian Edition: **Santa Teresa di Lisieux** - ISBN 978-88-6124-063-6, published by Il Pozzo di Giacobbe, Corso Vittorio Emanuele 32/34, 91100 Trapani (TP), Italy © 2008 Crispino di Girolamo.

A LITTLE FLOWER

Thérèse was born on 2nd January 1873 into a prosperous and religious family. Her father was a watchmaker named Louis Martin, and her mother was called Marie-Azélie Guérin. They already had four other daughters: Marie, Pauline, Léonie, and Céline. Thérèse was the youngest, and was well looked after as she grew up. Outside her large house, there was a lovely garden where Thérèse and her sisters spent a lot of time playing and looking after the flowers. She felt just like a flower herself, one of the small and common ones. Everyone loved her, and her early life was full of warmth and joy.

PAULINE HER 'MOTHER'

When Thérèse was just four years old, something very sad happened to her family: her mother Zélie died. The daughters, who were sad because of the loss of their mother, tried to help, support and encourage each other. The eldest, Pauline, began to care for Thérèse, who still needed a lot of attention and looking after. Pauline became a second mother for her, and the relationship between the two became very close.

Thérèse was a sensitive girl, but Pauline knew how to take care of her: she was patient with her sister, and tried to help her when times were hard. When Thérèse was unwell Pauline looked after her with kindness, and if she was sad her sister took her into the garden. Sometimes, they even went for rides in the wheelbarrow! Thérèse loved her and became more and more attached to her.

Pauline listened to her little sister and answered all her questions. One day Thérèse asked, "How come some saints are greater than others and receive more glory from God? Doesn't it make the lesser saints unhappy?" So Pauline took the glass their father drank from, and the small cup Thérèse used and told her: "Fill them both up with water."

"Now," she said once Thérèse had filled them both, "Which one is fuller?"

Thérèse answered, "Both of them are full!"

"It is the same with people," Pauline said, "God gives each person enough to fill them… The saints are all happy, because they all gave everything they had to God, and received everything they could from him."

THINKING OF GOD

It had been clear for some time that Pauline wanted to enter a Carmelite convent, and in the family, they talked a lot about what she wanted to do, and about when she would enter the religious life.

Thérèse listened carefully to all the talk going on within the family about Pauline, who had become very important for her.

All the family had a very pious upbringing and little Thérèse wanted to follow the example of her older sisters: she waited for them to come back from hearing Mass and they would tell her what they listened to in Church, and she wanted to be with them when they prayed, even though she was not yet able to take part. Thérèse was also very moved by her sister Céline's First Holy Communion. Even though she was little, Thérèse found ways to be like her sisters, and day by day, the wish to be with God and be consecrated to him, like her sister Pauline, grew stronger.

One day, the teacher at the abbey where Thérèse was attending school asked her what she did during the holidays.

Thérèse answered, "I go into my room, close the curtains and sit behind my bed, where there is a little space, just for me."

"And then what do you do?"

"I sit and think."

"And what do you think about?"

"I think about God, about life and about heaven," Thérèse told her.

A SPECIAL DAY

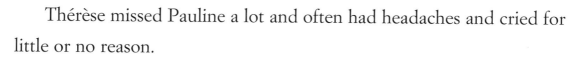

When Pauline entered the convent, Thérèse was nine years old. She knew it was an important step for her sister, and that Pauline would be happy in the convent, but it was hard for Thérèse to be without her. Céline became her closest companion, as all her sisters did their best to help her.

Thérèse missed Pauline a lot and often had headaches and cried for little or no reason.

From the convent, Pauline watched over her sister, sending her notes and letters each week, to encourage her. When the time for Thérèse's First Communion arrived, an event she had been preparing for with great solemnity with the help of her sister Marie, Pauline sent her a beautiful little book, full of pictures and images.

Thérèse was overwhelmed with joy on the day of her First Holy Communion. When she received Christ in the consecrated host, Thérèse felt "like a drop in the sea." An infinite love surrounded her and held her. Thérèse said she felt the "kiss" of Jesus.

There was a great celebration in the family for her Communion, but the most beautiful moment was when they all went to see Pauline at the Carmelite convent. When Thérèse met her sister, she was pleased to see that both of them were wearing a white veil. Thérèse was wearing the veil because of her Communion, and Pauline was wearing the veil because she was preparing to be married to Jesus.

A GIFT FROM JESUS

After Pauline, Marie also entered the convent and the desire to do the same continued to grow in Thérèse.

Though she got older, her character remained fragile. She cried often and was affected by everything that happened around her. Despite this, she still wanted to become a nun. Thérèse knew something was not quite right, because the decision to become a nun is an important one, whereas she often behaved like a little girl. But help came to her in a very special moment.

During midnight Mass of Christmas 1886, Thérèse heard Jesus call her, and something changed inside her. She felt loved and consoled. The death of her mother and the absence of her sister did not hurt her anymore. It seemed her tears had been dried and her weakness and fragility taken away.

Finally, she felt strong and courageous. It was a gift which Jesus the Son of God had given to her, he who became small so that little ones like her could reach heaven. Thérèse understood that faith is a gift, and does not depend on how good a person is.

When she was older, Thérèse called that night, the moment of her conversion.

ABOVE ALL THINGS

Thérèse's vocation was now clear to her, and she spoke of it often to Céline, who always encouraged her. Her faith grew and became stronger. She received the sacraments and read Holy Scripture and other important holy books whenever she could. Thérèse had many books and carried them with her everywhere, into the garden or during her travels.

After some time, she decided to tell her father that she intended to follow her sisters into the convent. She chose a moment when they were alone, outside in their lovely garden. Her father was moved by the words of his youngest daughter, and though he knew she was still little, he felt her desire was real.

So they went for a walk and he picked a little white flower for her, saying, "Look Thérèse, can you see how beautiful this simple little flower is? Think with what care God has made it and helped it to grow. That's what he has done for you too."

Thérèse was glad her father agreed with her decision, and in order to remember the moment, she took the flower, and put it in the centre of a book and looked after it like something very precious. The page she chose for the flower began with the words, "Loving God above all things."

ON PILGRIMAGE

But there was still a long way to go because Thérèse was still young. She was only 14 when she first asked to enter the convent, but the superiors told her to wait. Thérèse was sad, she wrote to her sister Pauline saying she was upset at not being allowed to enter the convent. Her sister encouraged her but asked her to be patient.

In 1887 Thérèse, her father and her sister Céline, went on a pilgrimage to Italy. On their way to Rome they visited many towns, including Milan, Florence and Loreto, seeing the cathedrals and holy places each city had. They even arranged to go to an audience with Pope Leo XIII when they got to Rome. Thérèse was glad because she wanted to ask the Pope himself to allow her to enter the convent even though she was too young.

While they crossed the Alps, Thérèse spent much of the time looking out of the window of their carriage, at the mountains, trees and green valleys. The thing she loved to look at most was the snow. While she looked, Thérèse thought of the marvels that there are in creation. She also thought that when she entered the convent she would only be able to see one corner of the sky from her window, but this neither frightened nor upset her.

When they finally arrived in Rome, Thérèse addressed her question to Pope Leo XIII, who replied, "If it is God's will, you will enter the convent." But she had wanted a more definite answer and was disappointed. She returned home knowing that this waiting period was only a test.

LIKE THE SNOW

Finally, in 1888 at the age of 15, Thérèse was allowed to enter the convent. The night before going, she found herself seated around the dinner table with all her family. It was the last time she sat with all those dear to her. The next day, on the 9th April, Thérèse went to stay in the convent. She found everything beautiful, and exactly as she had imagined it: the discipline, prayer and work. Thérèse felt it was the place for her and a new peace came into her heart. The months passed and Thérèse's day of vestiture (when she would put on the proper habit for the first time) approached.

Meanwhile, her father had become ill, with all the sisters worried for him. The day of vestiture was postponed.

When her father had recovered, Thérèse put on the habit in January 1889, it was the time of her engagement to Jesus and she was overjoyed. When she woke on that morning, she saw something through the window that made her even happier, everything was covered in snow.

It seemed to Thérèse, that on that special day, nature too wanted to put on white, just as she would.

After the ceremony, Thérèse embraced her father and went back into the convent. The first thing she saw, was a statue of the baby Jesus. The nuns kept the statue in a special place surrounded by lights and flowers. She stopped and thought she saw him smile at her surrounded by the snow.

Later, when she made her profession she took the name Thérèse of the Child Jesus.

THE LITTLE WAY

Life continued calmly in the Carmelite convent. It was a simple life of sharing prayer and work. Together with another nun, Thérèse looked after the novices. She loved the little things, she knew God was everywhere and gave himself in everything, so she never missed an opportunity to do good and grow in faith.

This is what Thérèse called "The Little Way": a path that did not require heroic efforts, nor great renunciations: a way everyone can walk, doing God's will in their lives. "The Little Way" meant doing what needed to be done in any particular moment, while leaving space for love in the small things that make up life.

As time passed, Thérèse understood that her only task was to love. She wrote, "My vocation is to love. I want to be the love in the heart of the Church."

Even though she did everything required by the Carmelite Rule, Thérèse preferred to read the Scriptures and do good deeds in secret, like helping sisters who were sad or giving anyone who was making her suffer, a smile.

Thérèse wrote one day that we are all like flowers in a large garden that are different in form, size and scent. There is the splendid rose, the noble lily, and the little daisy. That, Thérèse said, is how God sees his children, all beautiful in their own way, and he loves them as they are.

THÉRÈSE AND THE MISSIONS

In 1894, a painful moment arrived for Thérèse; her father died. Her sister Céline, who had been looking after him, entered the convent soon after. Thérèse too became ill, even though she was young. She became weak and had problems breathing. The first signs of her illness came in Holy Week of 1896. Despite her difficulties, Thérèse continued working with enthusiasm.

When she entered the convent, her work was to save souls and pray for priests. Like her namesake Teresa of Avila, she was always close to the life and work of missionaries who, with generosity overcame all sorts of obstacles, trying to bring the Gospel to all.

When she was given the task of praying for two missionaries, she was very happy. She wrote lovely letters, encouraging them, assuring them of her prayers for their mission. She took them as brothers, and felt near to them in her heart, despite not leaving the convent!

One day, there was the chance of Thérèse being sent to the new convent in Hanoi in Vietnam. She wanted very much to go. Her bad state of health, however, would not permit her to go on such a long journey, and she understood that her place was in Lisieux. She continued to write to, and pray for her brother missionaries.

When her illness got worse, Thérèse wrote to one of them, "If I go to heaven, I will ask Jesus if I can come and visit you, so we can continue your work together."

THE SLEEP OF CHRIST

The last year of her life was the hardest for Thérèse. It was not just her illness that caused her problems. During this time, she went through what people who do not believe in God go through. It was a spiritual suffering, she felt surrounded by darkness and Jesus seemed far away. Thérèse felt that this pain brought her closer to those who were in need of salvation. In her heart she knew, Jesus was nearer to her then, than he had ever been before. She remembered the Gospel story where Jesus is asleep in the boat and his apostles are frightened by the storm. She remembered that he woke up and saved his friends.

When Thérèse understood that Jesus had not abandoned her but was deep in her heart, she stopped being afraid, and stopped suffering.

She wrote, "Christ is asleep in my little boat, but this does not make me sad, it makes me happy."

Thérèse died on 30th September 1897 aged 24. She left many writings behind, including her autobiography, "The story of a soul," more than 200 letters, many poems, prayers and compositions.

She was venerated immediately after her death and devotion to her spread far and wide.

Thérèse was canonised in 1925, proclaimed patron saint of missions in 1927 and declared a Doctor of the Church on 19th October 1997.

SOME OF THÉRÈSE'S THOUGHTS

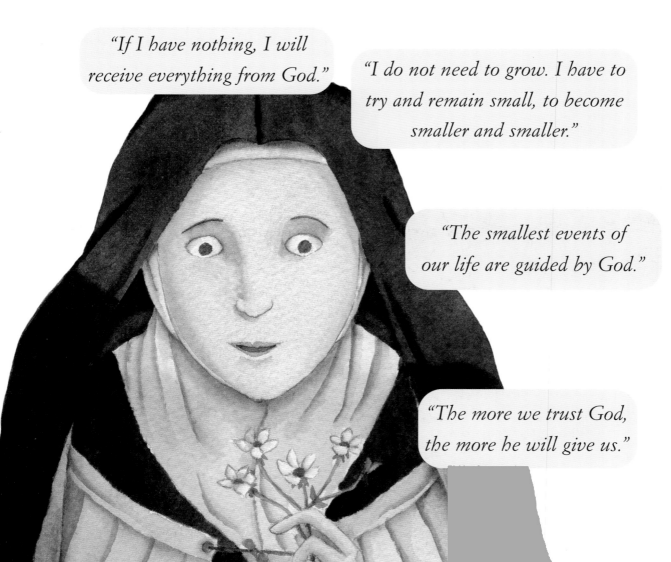